GEMS OF MYSTICISM

Teachings of

The Order of Christian Mystics

GEMS OF MYSTICISM

Teachings of The Order of Christian Mystics

The "Curtiss Books" freely available at

www.orderofchristianmystics.co.za

1 The Voice of Isis
2 The Message of Aquaria
3 The Inner Radiance
4 Realms of the Living Dead
5 Coming World Changes
6 The Key to the Universe
7 The Key of Destiny
8 Letters from the Teacher Volume I
9 Letters from the Teacher Volume II
10 The Truth about Evolution and the Bible
11 The Philosophy of War
12 Personal Survival
13 The Pattern Life
14 Four-Fold Health
15 Vitamins
16 Why Are We Here?
17 Reincarnation
18 For Young Souls
19 Gems of Mysticism
20 The Temple of Silence
21 The Divine Mother
22 The Soundless Sound
23 The Mystic Life
24 The Love of Rabiacca
25 Potent Prayers

Supporting Volumes

26 The Seventh Seal
27 Towards the Light

GEMS OF MYSTICISM

The fundamental teaching of this Order is that in every Soul there is a Divine Guidance which, if the human personality will listen, will clearly indicate that which is right and wrong.

Selected from the Writings of DR. & MRS. F. HOMER CURTISS
Founders of the Order of Christian Mystics

We aim to help all to find the Jewel of Truth in the mire of their existence, and to make their lives more tolerable because less mysterious and crushing.

Compiled by F. K. Davis

2015 EDITION

REPUBLISHED FOR THE ORDER BY
MOUNT LINDEN PUBLISHING
JOHANNESBURG, SOUTH AFRICA
ISBN: 978-1-920483-03-6

"Ministers of Christ and Stewards of the Mysteries of God."

1 Corinthians 4 vs. 1

BY
MOUNT LINDEN PUBLISHING

First Published in 1920

INDEX

GEMS OF MYSTICISM[1,2]

FOREWORD

"Golden in their wisdom and luminous with love, the treasured thoughts grouped herein have been to me as life itself.

Meditate on them in gratitude and they shall give you Light in the hour of darkness, Courage in defeat, Faith in time of trial, Patience in adversity, Love when beset by hate, Wisdom in the midst of error, and *the Key to find the Master whom you seek.*

Where your secret thought is, there are you.

Let this little book guide you into the Gates of Wisdom—aye, to the Heart of Love itself."

Forest K. Davis

---

[1] Curtiss, *Gems of Mysticism*

[2] Many of these quotations are from lessons which have never been published and are at time of this publishing, unavailable.

Chapter 1

SPIRITUAL GROWTH

It is not what your hands are doing, but *what your heart is worshiping* that determines your growth.

The Voice of Isis, p33

In every heart there is a well so deep and still that it can reflect only one star at a time, and this star, whatever it be, is, for the time it is reflected there, the guiding star of your destiny.

The Voice of Isis, p36

To think much about your shortcomings and limitations is but to give them life and force, for thoughts are things and create after their kind. Determine to think strength, love and confidence until you draw them to you and build them into your life.

Letters from the Teacher Vol I, p108

If you stumble, do not waste a moment's thought over it, but remember the lesson from it and say: "I must be up and doing. That is past and gone and it shall not hold me back." Truly nothing can hold you back unless you hold to it. If you were running a race and tripped and fell, would you waste time carefully inspecting the spot where you fell and wondering how it happened? No! You would be up and on, intent only on reaching the goal, not even conscious of the bruises you had received. Thus must you run the race which ends in Mastery.

The Voice of Isis, p133

To reach Mastery each Soul must live up to the light and the conceptions of Truth as revealed to him in his own religion, nation and environment.

The Voice of Isis, p399

The Path (to Mastery) is the Path of Renunciation; it is also a path of glorious achievement. Upon it you will find many things to comfort you during the long nights of darkness and the days of combat, many resting places, many joys. . . . The renunciation must be the renunciation of the dominion of the lower self and the discipline and training of its desires and appetites.

The Voice of Isis, p296

No one can claim to give spiritual development. Only the Soul itself can earn it.

Letters from the Teacher Vol I, p10

Spiritual growth is not a matter of what goes into the stomach, but of the devotion with which you live out the ideals of your heart. Each one, however, is responsible for the condition of all his bodies and must give them due attention, the attention necessary to keep any high-bred animal, of which high-grade work is expected, in good physical condition.

The Voice of Isis, p397

Just go about your Father's business each day accomplishing the tasks that are yours. . . . each day doing the little things, bright-eyed, clear-visioned, and with a cheerful countenance, seeing the stones and ruts in your path, but able to see how to step over or around them because the Light within your heart has become the light of your world, combining Love and Wisdom.

The Inner Radiance, pp185-186

Every positive stand you take builds character, increases your strength, lifts you out of your negative state, gives you power to conquer your weaknesses and tends to make promptness, courage, resolution and trust habits which will replace the negative habit of making excuses.

The Key of Destiny, p242

Seek earnestly for the particular line of teaching which most appeals to you and which proves most helpful to your spiritual growth, then, while recognizing the good in all others and being tolerant of all divergent views, be well-grounded in your chosen teaching, so that you cannot be misled or carried away by sophistry, but will remain unmoved as long as the teaching feeds your spiritual hunger.

The Voice of Isis, p298

If you bask in the Sun of Righteousness to keep from growing normally would be impossible. Learn to love, and forget. Become so interested in works of mercy and helpfulness that you will know that you are growing only by the perfume of good that surrounds you and by your increased ability to help others.

Letters from the Teacher Vol I, p106

Your life must be an unfolding of that which you, and no one else, are intended to be. Hence you cannot judge or lay down laws for another. Never seek merely to copy another or to gather the forces which belong to another, but recognize and build into your character the germs of good to be found in every thing, within yourself and within your environment. Without the perfection of your character the whole plan of the Universe would lack. If you consciously redeem and uplift every mistake, fault or experience, your life will be a continual unfolding from within by a utilization of that which is without, rather than a vain striving to copy or be something which you are not. But in this unfoldment seek diligently to find the germs of that which the Real Self is trying to manifest, else you will be but building up a mental conception of what you think you should be and ignoring those characteristics which are really you.

The Lord Jesus Christ, II, p3

There is no royal road to Divine Wisdom. There is, however, a straight and narrow path to spiritual unfoldment. It is found only by wedding Knowledge to Understanding and Love to Wisdom. It must be trodden step by step, often in weariness and with bleeding feet.

The Voice of Isis, p280

If we control one selfish trait which before held us captive, we may know that we have taken a real step upward. And the first and greatest of all magical powers to be attained by the pupil is the magical power of controlling himself; of day after day mastering the little things, with no heroics, perhaps with no one to commend him or realize that he is making any effort, yet still controlling his little tempers, his little impatience's, little acts of selfishness, his tendency to criticize, and all the little, trifling things he knows are wrong, but which seem too petty to be worth mentioning. . . . The building of these little lessons into his life is the most "practical" formula that can be given him.

The Voice of Isis, pp382-383

Victory over discouragement is one of the greatest victories man can win.

The Voice of Isis, p45

Have you no confidence in the love and power of the great Masters of Wisdom to protect and sustain you when you study Their teachings or would be about Their business?

The Key of Destiny, p242

Words are sacred things though few there be who realize it. Words should be to thought what steam is to the engine; if directed to the cylinder and flywheel the engine does perfect work, but if the steam escapes through many tiny holes and cracks, the power available for real work is diminished and wasted steam, like idle words, is an indication of dissipated power. . . . Do not consider them idle, however, even if apparently trifling and foolish, provided they bring cheer and comfort into the life of some other. They are only idle when wasted in mere talking instead of doing.

Letters from the Teacher Vol I, p108

Think what one kind word can do! How it can bring sunshine and peace and courage into your own life and the lives of others! Waste no force in frivolous or negative chatter; speak only positive words, words of love, words of power. If your brother offend you, speak words of love that your heart may send back nothing but love. Never withhold a sincere word of love or endearment, or a word of help, encouragement or health. A kind word spoken even to a stray dog will not return to you void. We cannot emphasize too strongly this fact: "That every idle word (either spoken or written) that men shall speak, they shall give account thereof in the day of judgment."

The Voice of Isis, pp175-176

Do not criticize others, even though your criticism seems just, for to do so you must dwell mentally in the conditions you criticize.

The Voice of Isis, p385

Shut out destructive, disintegrating thoughts; refuse to give them added life and power. Think only vital, helpful, cheerful, constructive thoughts. Speak only wise, loving, cheerful, helpful words.

The Great Book, p2

To control sensation is the first step toward Mastery. Until this step has been taken all others are barred by the very laws of Nature, for the seat of sensation is in the astral body, which is the path of communication between the physical and the spiritual.

Letters from the Teacher Vol I, p124

If you go through life with desire instead of Will for motive power, spiritually you are drifting aimlessly with the tide. And there is no more hopeless person than one who merely desires to be good, desires to be liberal, to be happy, to be thought well of, yet who makes no definite effort of Will to attain his ideal. . . . Make your life forceful, with Will standing back of everything you do or think. But at the same time draw close and let the mother-love pervade and bring forth the Christ in you, so that all who meet you will recognize that while you are positive and forceful, you are also loving. Better is he who with an open mind Wills to do and makes a mistake, than he who stands still or drifts along on the exhaust steam of desire. For if he is earnestly pressing forward, the imperfect or mistaken attainment of today will be left behind without a sigh tomorrow, for the advance he has made will give him a fuller understanding and a greater appreciation of what is best for his spiritual unfoldment and he will see his goal draw closer and closer as he draws closer and closer to the perfect manifestation of Divine Will and Love.

The Message of Aquaria, pp70-72

Each can help himself best by helping all humanity; for as Nature abhors a vacuum, the more love and purity you pour out for humanity, the more rushes in to take its place.

The Voice of Isis, p268

Love is the one and only reality which endures from eternity to eternity. . . . In nature, water is the chief factor which makes the earth bring forth, while in man that which is symbolized by water, the Great Mother principle (Love), brings forth spiritual fruits.

The Voice of Isis, pp46-47, 198

All temptations met with on the Path come through various aspects of Love, even Jesus in the wilderness being obliged to face and conquer the love of power, dominion and ambition. On earth we see Love manifesting as love of gold, love of power, love of self, love of pleasure, love of animal gratification and so forth, all perverted or negative polarizations of Divine Love.

The Voice of Isis, p197

When it is once grasped that the working out of a personal salvation is the only way really to help the world, the man who neglects it is a retarder of the public good.

Letters from the Teacher Vol I, p125

Many pupils ask for something practical to do to develop occult powers and manifest the higher life. Noting the effect of your words is practical and most important, and until at least some conception of the power of speaking kindly and lovingly but to some purpose, and some degree of mastery over it has been attained, the development of all other occult powers will be retarded, if not actually prevented.

The Voice of Isis, p175

Since man is the microcosm of the macrocosm, in his spiritual evolution he must pass through stages analogous both to his own physical evolution and that of the planet, just as during his inter-uterine life he passes through the evolutionary stages of the early races, vegetative, animal, human.

The Voice of Isis, p210

Let each Soul take the little grains of experience in his or her nature, learn the lessons from them and build round them layer after layer of love and devotion until they become pearls of Wisdom.

The Message of Aquaria, p261

Many declare they find it impossible to live out their true selves; but the inner development will always manifest, no matter what the environment. If a Soul fails to demonstrate that it is spiritually advanced it simply means that it has not attained to or created the state that it desires to manifest. If one is absorbed in petty cares, to the exclusion of higher aims, it means that he has not outgrown petty conditions; for if he had he would find time to follow the higher leadings and manifest them in his life.

The Voice of Isis, p275-276

The battle is not one-sided. In fact, "He that is with you (your Higher Self) is greater than he (the personality or lower self) that is against you."

The Voice of Isis, p92

He who says he has realized the Divine within himself, yet only as power for his own upliftment, and who uses it only for his own advancement, has never even approached that realization.

The Voice of Isis, p73

The first Gate to be passed is the attainment of Charity and Tolerance for all; a realization of Divine Love, and an earnest desire to become one with The Christ-force which is manifesting in your fellow man. This is the first Gate to be entered because intolerance is a bar to further progress.

The Voice of Isis, p297

An important point to remember, is not to copy the actions of others or try to square your life with the ideals of others, but bravely seek deep within your own being for the germs of action implanted in the personality by the Higher Self and make the personality measure up to the ideal given you by your own Higher Self. In other words, find yourself, do your own thinking, and live true to your own divine guidance.

The Voice of Isis, p132

Before the student can receive spiritual illumination all old conceptions or coverings to his understanding must be put off or laid aside that the understanding may receive the Light direct.

The Voice of Isis, p317

You are often told to live close to Nature, yet very few understand the significance of that injunction. . . . To live close to Nature is to feel your oneness with her; to realize that the same forces are operating in you, in your body, in your mind, in your spiritual life, as in the verdant hills and budding trees. It does not necessarily mean living in a tent or sleeping on the ground, but it does mean correlating your consciousness with Nature, trying through meditation to enter the phases of natural growth and development, recognizing the similarity and the oneness of all growth.

Letters from the Teacher Vol I, pp112, 113

In Nature you will find an explanation of every experience through which you pass.

Letters from the Teacher Vol I, p112

It is just as selfish to permit your humility to occupy the foreground in your thoughts and continually impose it upon the thoughts of others, as continually to seek your own pleasure.

The Voice of Isis, p132

What would be a slight lapse from virtue in a savage or in the ignorant, becomes a cyclone of iniquity, sweeping many before it, in one who has entered the inner degrees of occultism; for upon each inner step every vibration is multiplied a thousand fold. The disciple should absolutely master (gain perfect control of, not suppress) all life-forces ere he attempts to enter the inner degrees, or his failure is foreordained.

The Voice of Isis, p251

Truth is more than merely refraining from speaking falsely. It means being true in every phase of your thoughts, desires and life, being true to your Divine Self. Let Truth search out every hidden fault and failing that you may recognize and correct it. Have no false conceptions, no veils to hide your real character from you. Above all things be true. Think true. Act true. Live true.

The Key of Destiny, p314

Chapter 2

DUTY

The first duty of each student of the higher life is to make a careful analysis and decide what are real and what are superficial duties, then so to order his life that the real, vital and first duty of caring for his Immortal Soul will not be crowded out.

The Voice of Isis, p30

The mustard seed grows into a mustard tree, with all its healing and medicinal qualities; the Rose develops into the queen of all flowers, giving out its refreshing perfume, the symbol of love, to all. The spiritual lesson is that both grow and unfold by merely doing the duty that lies nearest, that which is next at hand. They assimilate the earth-forces, the water, the air and the sun. Go thou and do likewise.

Letters from the Teacher Vol I, p107

It would be impossible for you to take one step onward while you were leaving any real duty undone.

The Voice of Isis, p30

All real duties confront you because in your evolution you have set up conditions which make just such tasks necessary to build into your Soul certain qualities in which you are lacking. . . . and without the lessons they teach your character is incomplete. Hence they are the things which, when they are performed and the qualities they are meant to develop are incorporated into your being, will give you the strength and ability to take your next step.

The Voice of Isis, pp30-31

If you perform a duty because you are compelled to, and fail to incorporate its lesson in your heart, at your next step you will find yourself confronted by another duty of the same general character but far more difficult of performance, and this will continue until you not only perform the duty, but gain the lacking quality of Soul this duty is intended to inculcate.

The Voice of Isis, p31

Take the little duties as they come, for not one step can be missed.

Letters from the Teacher Vol I, p107

There is no duty higher than the one which lies nearest, provided it be a real one.

The Voice of Isis, p33

Your body is the Temple of the Living God. It is your duty to see that in every way it is kept a fit dwelling place for the God within. The chief requisite for this is absolute purity of body, mind and heart. No natural function of the body but is pure and wholesome when used for its proper purpose. No natural act is, of itself, impure. It becomes impure only through impure thoughts concerning it. Not alone impure acts but also impure thoughts, even if only subconsciously held, are a source of defilement. The whole problem rests upon your ability to purify your thoughts concerning all the forces and functions of your bodies.

The Voice of Isis, p215, 217

It is not a real duty to try to relieve another from doing his plain duty.

The Voice of Isis, p33

Know well the burdens of all Souls are sent in Love. Deprive them not of the strength they bring, lest, alas, for lack of the burdens you would bear they should lose the prize.

The Soundless Sound, p27

Since all real duties are your task, in them lies your opportunity, and in their proper performance lies your victory. Not in the performance merely, but in the attitude of mind you hold toward them and the manner of their performance.

The Voice of Isis, p31

There is one real duty which confronts all students of the higher life that cannot be ignored, i. e., to decide just what avenue of help is most beneficial, not only to their own advancement, but also the one which brings the greatest amount of practical help to humanity. Hence, your first duty is conscientiously, prayerfully and earnestly to seek for the special channel through which you desire to help humanity, and when found throw into that channel all you have to give, whether it be money, the easiest of all things to give, or love, devotion and thought, or service.

The Voice of Isis, p32

Chapter 3

KARMA

KARMA is the implacable Law of Cause and Effect, bringing to you in exact justice the net results of your past thoughts, desires and acts, but it does not do so in detail and hence is not the Nemesis it is so frequently represented to be. "For the only decree of Karma, an eternal and immutable decree, is absolute Harmony in the world of Matter as it is in the world of Spirit." It is not your acts that are the cause of your Karma, but the possession or lack of certain Soul-qualities which is the cause of your thoughts, desires and acts, whose effects are brought to you by the great Law of Harmony for readjustment. Disobedience to the Divine Law is not punished but is adjusted, even though the adjustment brings about sorrow and suffering. Everything that comes to you as trouble or sorrow is simply the result of your own shortcomings, your failure to learn the lessons which less painful experiences should have taught you. The main idea of Karma, then, is not one of punishment for past failures, but that you may learn your lesson and gain as quickly as possible the Soul-qualities needed, that you may fulfil your destiny, your special place and work in the Grand Plan.

The Voice of Isis, pp115, 117

Know ye not the conditions of life in which you find yourself are those best fitted for your Soul-growth?

The Soundless Sound, p23

The adjustment of Karma is brought about consciously through spiritual attainment.

Letters from the Teacher Vol I, p42

If you refuse to recognize the lesson, or run away from the conditions ere they are conquered, you will have to meet them again and again in various forms in this and other lives until victory is gained.

The Voice of Isis, p34

The Law works as compensation in that in every experience, be it painful or otherwise, there is a compensating power to be gained or a reward which is well worth the suffering necessary to build it into Soul-growth. Inextricably blended with the Law as Compensation is that aspect known as Karma. That is, effects of causes set up in previous times or former lives are brought to you in orderly sequence to be worked out, and in turn to set up fresh causes. The great point to understand in this manifestation of the Law is that Karma is neither a reward nor a punishment for past deeds, and still less is it an avenging Nemesis remorselessly exacting "an eye for an eye and a tooth for a tooth", but is the effect of causes in the sense that it brings to the Soul the opportunity to learn certain lessons which it has not learned in a past life, hence which the Law of Love brings to it through this manifestation that it may gain the Soul-quality needed for further progress.

The Voice of Isis, pp194-195

No matter what the burden laid upon you, it is not laid there merely that you may suffer, nor does any God wish you to bear it. It is yours because somewhere, sometime, you missed a lesson in life that only such a burden could teach you. Therefore, conditions worked together and you were brought face to face with your lesson. Try to realize this. Then, if you can admit that what you are forced to bear is meant merely as a lesson to point out some shortcoming or absolute fault, know well that the moment you learn the lesson or correct the fault the experience will no longer be needed and it will pass away.

Letters from the Teacher Vol I, p111

Whatever the condition that confronts you, know well that it will never leave you until you have gained the Wisdom it is intended to teach.

The Voice of Isis, p34

Do not rail at your experiences or conditions of life, but rather welcome them as opportunities to gain new lessons, experiences whose mastery will give you added strength and understanding. Do not fight or fear conditions but welcome them; for the thing you fear exhausts you, while the thing you welcome yields you its strength and power.

The Christ, p3

There is only one way effectually to bring about a better condition, and that is to recognize that you are where you are because the Soul, or Higher Self, realizes that there is some important lesson to learn which those conditions can teach better than any other, and set to work to learn that lesson. Realize that conditions do not really retard, but are intended to make you think and take account of stock. First, try to determine what lesson you must learn, then take it determinedly to heart until you have conquered. We know that no man has conditions given to him that he does not need, and that the moment he gets out of a condition, its highest good, he is rid of it forever.

Letters from the Teacher Vol I, pp118-119

Try to realize that when bound on the Wheel of Karma, to struggle but makes the cords cut deeper into your quivering flesh. Stop struggling. Lo! I say unto you: Peace, be still. All is well. Learn the lesson of saying, "Thy will be done," knowing that the Will of the Father is victory and that it will and must be done.

Letters from the Teacher Vol I, pp107-108

If the Soul were obliged to reap all the Karma in one life that it had generated in the last preceding life there would be neither time nor opportunity for progress. Therefore, the Lords of Light hold back a certain percentage from each life, and manipulate the currents of force so that a chance is given the Soul to learn the main lesson of the last earth life and at the same time have an opportunity to gain entirely new experiences. But, before final liberation can come, each Soul must, of its own choice, take up all the accumulated odds and ends of Karma and work them out or redeem them.

Letters from the Teacher Vol I, p48

Just as the grosser flame sweeps the forest, so the subtler "fire of the Lord" or the fire of the Law (Karma), before which the earthly man is but chaff, sweeps humanity. The flames that consume the debris, the underbrush and the twining parasites which sap the vitality of the giant trees also cause new vegetation to spring up. Likewise in our hearts after we have passed through a karmic burning we find new and unexpected manifestations of life and growth. Think of the burnings of karmic Law not as something to which you must school yourself, something that will deprive you of every happiness, take from you your cherished ideals and bring naught but desolation, but think of it in its constructive aspect. Realize that just as the heat and life and light of the sun penetrate the earth to bring forth the seeds, so shall these subtle fires of Karma sink deep into your heart and germinate all the seeds of immortal power which you have stored up in past incarnations and which only await the fire to sweep away old conditions, everything that interferes with your spiritual growth, to germinate and put forth. Declare yourself ready to stand in the burnings of the Law, not passively giving up because it is your Karma, but that your heart and mind and life, all that is manifested on all planes, may be purified and make way for the new spiritual growth.

Fire of the Law, pp2-4

A golden vessel to be placed upon the King's table must pass through a seven-times heated furnace and be hammered and tested and purified until the gold is without a flaw; then it must be fashioned into the shape best adapted to its purpose. So it is with the vessel of clay which we call our personality.

The Voice of Isis, p35

Since all evolution tends to develop more and more perfect organisms through which greater and greater degrees of freedom from the bondage of external conditions can manifest, we can be truly free from the bonds of Karma only as we work with evolution through the seeking of those things which are our own and following those things which will perfect and thus hasten our evolution. This is not attained by selfishly trampling on the freedom or rights of others that we may advance, for to do so is to develop selfishness, but through harmonious co-operation for the good of all.

The Key to the Universe, p305

We do not mind bearing trials when we know that we are merely correcting mistakes made in a past life, or else learning needed lessons in this. Trials are not given as punishments, but as the only means of making us learn the lessons that will fit us to take our real places at the right hand of God-the-Father, and to gain a greater realization of His nearness and help while here below.

Letters from the Teacher Vol I, pp140-141

Understand clearly, whatever sicknesses, troubles or trials come to a person they are either the result of broken law or are conditions given by the Higher Self to teach certain necessary lessons and thus gain the experience needed to take the Soul a step onward. Often by pouring his personal magnetism (prana) into the aura of a patient, or by sheer force of Will, one may so influence another as temporarily to drive away sickness or trouble, but if the real lesson which the sickness or trouble was meant to teach has not been learned by the patient, the moment the will-power is withdrawn the trouble will return. Or, if the will-power has been strong enough, the trouble may be driven back off the physical-plane to appear upon some higher plane, perhaps in a different form such as some form of nervous disorder or mental trouble.

Letters from the Teacher Vol I, p77

All broken contracts and all disobedience to the Law produce inharmony on all planes at the same time. And the persons bringing into action the particular inharmonious note must themselves readjust every wave of inharmony that has been produced by their acts before harmony can be restored in their lives. This is a benign and beneficent law; for it is only by reaping what we have sown, and eating the fruits thereof, that we can ever learn to plant wheat instead of tares. It is not denial of inharmony that settles the score, but a recognition of it and the correction of its cause. If through will-power you push it aside and apparently gain either health, wealth or some other earthly comfort ere the readjustment is made, the inharmony will gather force by the very pushing back and will sweep over you again and again until it is recognized and adjusted. True healing combines all physical agencies with the psychic and the Divine, for these three are one.

Letters from the Teacher Vol I, pp77-78, 82

The pressure from without cannot harm you, if the within be properly balanced.

The Voice of Isis, p44

Every inharmony is continually working toward readjustment, just as all wounds tend to heal, and all forms of disease to cure themselves.

The Temple of Silence, pp25-26

As the conditions of life flow to it the Soul consciously gathers out of the varied experiences of life just those germs of good (lessons) that are needed to make it grow into the likeness of the perfected Being which that particular individual is destined to become.

The Lord Jesus Christ, II, p3

All seeds are planted in the earth, yet each seed grows into the particular plant whose germ and pattern are within. So each Soul is planted in the soil of its earthly environment, with the pattern of the perfect man to be embodied within the sheath of his personality. That which brings unrest and dissatisfaction is the effort and striving to manifest something that is not within.

The Iron Age, p4

How many would gladly attempt to bear the hardships and sufferings of their loved ones rather than stand aside and permit them to fulfil their karmic destiny in exact justice. But their loved ones cannot be purified and pass on to higher things, if their burdens are borne for them and they are not allowed to meet their tests and stand in the fiery furnace which they in ages past have lighted. Stand aside then, and while giving all love, sympathy and encouragement, allow all to meet their tests and burnings that they may be purified and advance to higher things.

The Voice of Isis, pp82-83

Every word we utter has not only its vibrations, but, together with the form, colour and number of the letters composing it, possesses a potency that will never die, but go on and on through the ages until we, their creator, by the power of The Christ within, shall have redeemed them. Be their power for good or ill, it forms one of the very considerable forces that go to make up the law of Karma. Suffering of itself has no purifying or uplifting power. It is uplifting only when the lesson which necessitated it has been learned and the lacking Soul-quality has been built into the character.

The Voice of Isis, pp39-40

Know absolutely, that the Law is, and that it must work out. If one jot or tittle of the Law could go wrong in your personal affairs, all creation would be thrown out of harmony.

Letters from the Teacher Vol I, p95

As you realize that it is yourself who is responsible for all the disturbing influences which surround you, and that it rests with you to overcome them by eliminating their causes, you have begun in the right way to work with the Law and gain Self-knowledge and Self-poise. Make yourself one with the Law and all its manifestations will work in harmony.

The Voice of Isis, p119

Bodily weakness should not be looked upon either as a failure or as a karmic debt, although in some cases it might be either or both. However, no matter what its immediate cause, it is a lesson. Often it is a needed lesson in patience and sympathy for suffering that locks the Soul in such a body, but more often it is a lesson that only a great Soul is ready to learn.

Letters from the Teacher Vol I, p74

You who weep; you who feel discouraged; lift up your hearts and know that today, in this very hour, the mighty forces from out the unknown are being poured out upon you. Open your heart and mind and receive them.

The Iron Age, p4

Chapter 4

REINCARNATION

No one is ready to learn the truth of reincarnation to whom it does not appeal. Only those who feel an inward urge to know the whole truth need have it given them. The whole object of rebirth is for each Soul to attain all-around Soul-perfection, learn all the lessons life can teach, and thus be prepared to do its work in the Grand Plan. Even if it were possible for a man to gain all knowledge and have all experience in one life, nevertheless the stupendous task of evolution, from an atom to a God, would require incalculable aeons. Comparing our life-period to a day, as well might we expect a child to acquire the experience and wisdom of a life-time between sunrise and sunset. . . . Perfection could not be attained in one life.

The Voice of Isis, p278

If each Soul were required to redeem in one life all its mistakes and spiritualize every atom with which it had been connected in even one life, the Cycle of Necessity would be never-ending. Instead of this all tasks that are beyond the strength of the Soul in any one incarnation are held back until it has grown strong enough little by little to work them out.

The Voice of Isis, p181

Each Soul is judged at the close of each life-cycle by the sum total of how much he has overcome, how much of the lower self he has illumined by the higher spiritual consciousness.

The Philosophy of War, 1st Ed., p24

The "I' is the Higher Self, the overshadowing Father-in-heaven. It is the True Self in that it is the Ego, a Spark of the Infinite, incarnating again and again in an animal body for the purpose of gaining experience in matter and, through its informing of physical atoms in an earthly body, to help redeem (spiritualize) matter. . . . The lower selves are like the outer husks of the seed which are dissolved and their substance indrawn to form nourishment for the seed, to enrich it and enable it to grow and blossom. . . . The body wears out and is cast aside just as a garment is, and a new one put on; but the Self never changes. It gains more experience and needs a better garment from time to time until, finally, it masters the matter which makes up its physical garments and immortalizes it so that the personality is swallowed up in the Individuality; the mortal puts on immortality and becomes one with its Father-in-heaven.

Letters from the Teacher Vol I, pp113-114, 122

Many ask, "Why is not the memory of past lives more common?" There is a deep reason for this. Most Souls find the memory of the trials of one life as much as the personality can bear, therefore the complete remembrance of all it had endured in its many lives would tend to crush it. It is memory that haunts; that drives to insanity. No one day can hold enough sorrow to dishearten utterly the personality; it is the accumulated burden that overwhelms. . . . therefore we will never be permitted to remember our past lives until we have advanced beyond the point where the grief's, the ills, and the unkindness done us can affect us, make us worry or become discouraged and thus retard our progress. We will not remember until we have gained that poise which nothing can disturb; until we have become centred in the thought that to manifest Divine Love in perfection is all that is worth striving for.

The Voice of Isis, pp270-271

The object of evolution is for mankind to gain Wisdom out of every condition.

The Voice of Isis, p34

CHAPTER 5

THE CHRIST

PRAYER FOR LIGHT

O CHRIST! Light Thou within my Heart the Flame of Divine Love and Wisdom, that I may dwell forever in the Radiance of Thy Countenance, and rest in the Light of Thy Smile!

The Mystic Christ is not a personality, but a Divine Essence. It is a spiritual emanation from the Godhead, the Son of God or the Godhead in its creative aspect; that Mystic Power or Principle which fructifies and animates all manifestations of life. It is the Divine Creative Force, a great stream of life-giving, creative Essence which manifests in all things on all planes as the animating Principle of the One Life.

The Mystic Christ, pp2-3

The Christ-force, therefore, is the animating Power back of all life and evolution, physical, mental, psychic, spiritual. In Nature it is the unquenchable urge toward perfection which adapts the organism to its environment. Among men it is the divine urge toward union with God; the effort "to bring the divine within them into harmony with the divine in the universe," as the mystic philosopher Plotinus expresses it.

The Mystic Christ, p3

It is this mystic, informing, vivifying Principle (The Christ-force), manifesting in and through Him, to which Jesus referred when He said : "I am the living bread which came down from heaven; if any man eat of this bread, he shall live forever: and the bread that I will give is my flesh, which I will give for the life of the world. . . . Whoso eateth my flesh, and drinketh my blood, hath eternal life." Manifestly such statements could not apply to any human flesh and blood, or even to an historical personality, but were used figuratively for that immortal, universal, mystic Principle which the personality of Jesus embodied. Eternal life cannot be obtained by merely observing or studying spiritual truths, for they must be eaten and assimilated into the nature, built into the character, made a part of the life, just as physical food must be assimilated to be built into the body, and manifest as love, tolerance, charity, brotherhood and purity, ere you have truly eaten of the body of The Christ.

The Mystic Christ, p4

Only as the Christ-force is embodied in you can you have eternal life. To grow spiritually it is not enough merely to lead ethical and morally blameless lives, but we must also drink of the blood and eat of the flesh of the Christ, i. e., drink in that spiritual creative Power or Divine Life-force which shall re-create us, which shall make our lives not merely automatic moral models, but dynamic, radiant centres of force for good, vibrant with that creativeness whose very emanations shall fructify and awaken in everything we contact an answering vibration and a quickened life. There must be an infusion of the creative life-force of The Christ into the personality until it becomes one with the Mystic Christ.

The Mystic Christ, p4

Difficulty arises through a failure to distinguish between the Mystic Christ-principle, which "hath shined in our hearts to give the knowledge of the glory of God," and the personality of the teacher Jesus who manifested an individualization of this Force to a superlative degree. This distinction is so plainly made throughout the New Testament that only the decadence of knowledge concerning the Mysteries and the lack of training in esoteric philosophy as a requirement for the ministry, can account for the utter ignoring of it and all that it implies.

The Mystic Christ, p1

In one sense the Gospel story of Jesus is meant to inspire those whose spiritual development requires a physical embodiment and a personal, historic example after which to pattern their lives. These are but children in spiritual understanding, to whom the beautiful embodiment of The Christ within the man Jesus, the Man of Sorrows, forms a picture with great emotional appeal. If they stop there, however, and are satisfied with the personality of the human teacher, they never really find The Christ as a personal, religious experience, nor do they even touch the hem of His garment. They worship but a picture and are doomed to disappointment and sorrow, for some day they must see their human Christ-ideal, as it exists today, crucified, cast down and destroyed. (By historical research, higher criticism, etc.) The literal, personal example or letter of the law, is not satisfying to the awakened Soul. The Pauline picture (of The Christ) is for those who need no historic personality as a model; those who open wide the doors of their hearts at the knock of the Mystic Christ; who can respond to the down pouring of Divine Love and through a divine ecstasy can enter into the higher realms of spiritual consciousness where the powers of the human mind are transcended and where they grasp those things which are spiritually discerned; those things which are "revealed unto his holy apostles and prophets by the Spirit."

The Mystic Christ, pp2-3

The story of the life of Jesus is not the personal history of one Great Teacher, but is an allegory of the life of perfected Man, the growth and perfection of the Soul, every incident symbolizing a step upon the Path of Attainment, from the birth of The Christ-consciousness in the heart of the personality, the weary pilgrimage of life, the crucifixion on the cross of matter and desire, to the glorious resurrection and ascension, when the personality has been perfected and The Christ-man sits at the right hand of the Father-in-heaven. In other words, when the personality of each of us has experienced the ascension and completed the at-one-ment with the Divine we become the right hand of the Father or the instrument through which His work is accomplished on earth. The story of

Jesus is the story of evolution. It is not the literal history of any one personality that is thus depicted, but the experiences which each Soul passes through as the Mystic Christ is born within and evolves to perfection or at-one-ment with its Father-in-heaven.

The Lord Jesus Christ, I, p2

When the name (Jesus) is coupled with The Christ (the word "the" having been eliminated as the distinction between the mystic Principle and its embodiment was lost to humanity) it stands for that stage in the growth of the Soul when the personality has made the at-one-ment with the Mystic Christ-principle, or, in theosophical terminology, the stage at which Manas has been blended with the Buddhic principle. For Manas is dual and in most cases the consciousness vacillates between the lower and the higher expression, functioning most of the time in the lower. The Jesus man becomes a Christ only when the human mind (Manas) is uplifted and blended with The Christ-consciousness (Buddhi and Atma, the Father-in-heaven) and the three become one or perfected Man. Hence the name of Jesus stands for the possibility of common, ordinary man, merging his personality into the Divine, entering The Christ-Consciousness and manifesting the Mystic Christ through his Jesus personality.

The Lord Jesus Christ, II, p2

It was expedient for you that your conception of the man Jesus perishing on the cross should go away, should be eliminated from your consciousness, that the Comforter, the Mystic Christ, might come to you, might enter into your heart and abide forever. Only through the Mystic Christ can you enter into a conscious oneness with the great Master Jesus, the guide, friend and Elder Brother of mankind.

The Lord Jesus Christ, II, p4

It makes very little difference, as far as the truth of His teachings is concerned, whether or not such a man as Jesus ever lived. As a matter of esoteric history, there was an Avatar of that name who did pass through the experiences symbolized in the Bible during the pilgrimage of His Soul toward mastery, just as every Soul must pass that way. But the whole story, as it is told, is one grand allegory designed to teach, exoterically, the inner truths of the different steps on the Path. Each step has its trials and sufferings, its mockery of the multitude and the final crucifixion of the lower personality and the glorious resurrection into life immortal, the triumph of the spiritual over the temporal man. The story is woven around this Avatar, Jesus, and events and places are adapted or created to carry out the symbology; but every name used, as well as every incident, has its inner meaning when interpreted kabalistically. This is the style after which all scriptures are written, i. e., The Vedas, Upanishads, etc. It is the method always adopted by Initiates in giving out the great truths so that only those who have developed the qualities necessary to the true understanding can see the inner meaning. The multitude see the beautiful story, which contains a sound moral lesson, and each one gets from it exactly what he is ready to receive.

Letters from the Teacher Vol I, pp12-13

You never know what you really are until the light of The Christ has illumined every corner of your being. Oft-times the unexpected beauty and strength revealed is quite as overwhelming as the shortcomings.

The Voice of Isis, p92

When the light of The Christ has illumined your heart and has awakened a recognition of your divine possibilities, it must also awaken all the latent propensities in your composite personality, for the same sun which causes the good seed to sprout in the garden of your heart will also stimulate in even greater profusion the growth of the weeds which, unless ruthlessly uprooted, will choke out the life of the good seed. Make no compromise. You must conquer or be overcome. For the very recognition of your divine birthright lashes into fury all those forces of your lower self which have held you in bondage so long.

The Voice of Isis, p91

Both intellectual development and heart development are necessary, but if the heart is first developed and a conscious union made with The Christ within, all things are revealed unto you. This is, as it were, the shortcut to Mastery.

The Voice of Isis, p384

The Christ. . . . is more than a Principle; is more than an entity or a force or a power; it is the manifestation of the Godhead. Yet it is entitized in every Master who has trodden the Way, manifested in Truth and discovered in Life. The Christ is a living power, the life of the Soul. It shines from the eyes, it emanates in waves of magnetic force from the fingertips; it shines as an aureole round about. It dwells within; it manifests without. . . . Through your own will and effort you must bring about the Resurrection of The Christ from the tomb of materiality. It is the density of matter that slows down the vibrations of this Principle, making it almost inactive. To you the task is given through the sublimating of the matter of your bodies to accomplish the resurrection of The Christ. . . . The Christ . . . is a manifestation of all that you can picture of a Divine Comforter; of a brother, a sister, a father, a mother. Who will come and stand beside Him upon the Rock of Truth? Who will cast from their lives, from their hearts, their stumbling-blocks? It matters not what the past holds. All that is gone before is like the water that has passed the water-wheel. It has turned it for good or for evil and the grain has been ground by its power. Some day you must come back and eat of its meal, but today you are past it. Therefore make today a day of Truth.

The Truth, pp1-3

The Christ-spirit is the cause of the eternal miracle of springtime, both in nature and in the Soul. It is a universal life-giving, all-powerful force that the human heart, as it lives and breathes and presses on in evolution, must imbibe and express more and more, even as nature imbibes and expresses the same Force in the springtime. It is Life itself, the essence of the Divine One Life. It is the perfume of the rose, the light of the sun, the nourishment of the food, the power of the breath, the sustaining quality of hope, the enduring quality of courage. In fact it is the Divine Spiritual Force that is back of all life, all thought and all experience.

The Christ Seed, p3

The great lesson of Easter is that each heart and life, in spite of all its faults and failings, is an effort of The Christ to manifest; that you are not inherently wicked or cursed from birth; that it is not a mighty struggle to evolve God-ward. It is simply a question of assimilating all the Light and Love poured out upon you and allowing The Christ Seed within to push up through the human personality and manifest its beauty and give its perfume to the world. Remember it will ultimately push up in spite of all you can do to retard it or deflect it, in spite of generations of opposition, in spite of war, in spite of so-called civilization, in spite of humanity's selfishness, self-will and determined perversity. Why not recognize its power now to transform and resurrect your life and help you to reach quickly the unfoldment that ultimately you cannot fail to reach? Why waste precious time and pass through unnecessary suffering when you can grow in peace, harmony and luxuriance if you will?

The Christ Seed, p4

The world is today awaiting the advent of a Divine Teacher or true Priest of the Lord, a personalized embodiment of the great Christos-principle of the universe, the all-pervading, vivifying power which underlies all manifestations of the One Life. As this great spiritual Being approaches the earth-plane each heart who can respond to the vibrations of His message will come more or less consciously into touch with Him, no matter what organization or movement he may be working in. . . .

The Message of Aquaria, p433

The cry of the Great One is now going forth to all who can hear: "Come unto me, my little lambs. The fold is waiting and the heart of the Shepherd yearning. Think of the thoughts that I have shed around you as you journeyed through the wilderness of lives and lives; think of the words that have been spoken through the mouths of my chosen prophets in your ears, life after life, age after age, and will ye still be deaf and dumb to love? To be sheep of my fold means to know your Shepherd, to gladly follow, to hear His voice and obey. Ah, my children, unless the sheep know the voice of the Shepherd they will be blind and will never recognize His face. Unless they learn to love and thus obey unquestioningly the divine message, they will never be ready to take their places in the Great Temple where the True Priesthood must work out the great scheme of salvation, the reflection upon earth of the Hierarchies of Heaven."

The Message of Aquaria, p435-436

CHAPTER 6

THE MASTERS OF WISDOM

The Masters of Wisdom are Great Souls who, through repeated experiences and determined effort through many earth lives, have obtained mastery, firstly, over the passions, appetites and desires of the personal self; and secondly, over the forces of Their bodies and over the life-currents of the Cosmos. Hence They have become one with the Fount of all Wisdom. They and the Father are one. Jesus was such a Master, in fact, was and is a Master of Masters. But there are many more, all banded together in what is known as The Great White Lodge; a lodge in the sense of oneness of aim and motive, for They are all working for the uplifting of humanity. They are divided into certain degrees and subdivided into orders so as to systematically cover all the needs of humanity in its different stages of evolution. You will thus see that there are Masters of all grades; that is, upon all steps of the ladder leading to the point of highest attainment where a Master of Masters stand. Each group and each individual has a certain work to do for the betterment of humanity. These Great Souls are able to function on all planes, hence They are near to all who really need Their help, for humanity must reach out for help ere it can be given.

Letters from the Teacher Vol I, p6

You can set it down as a positive fact that no Master of Wisdom ever did, ever will, or ever could advertise Himself or give out spiritual teachings at so much per lesson. Nor is there any such thing as an Initiate of the Great White Lodge upon the physical-plane acting in His physical body, and claiming to be such. The Great White Lodge does not work that way.

Letters from the Teacher Vol I, p10

As long as individuals are satisfied with a purely physical existence the Masters know well that they are not yet ready to be helped, for their lessons are those of the physical.

Letters from the Teacher Vol I, p6

The Masters of Wisdom know who need the outer help, and it never fails to present itself. It may seem to come from some natural and ordinary source, but in reality it is from these Watchers and Elder Brothers of humanity who make use of natural channels to answer the cry of the Soul for light and help.

Letters from the Teacher Vol I, p7

The Elder Brothers of humanity, the great Masters of Wisdom, into whose hands the evolution of the Race is entrusted, are continually sending forth the cry for helpers. "The harvest truly is great, but the labourers are few," for They can work on the earth-plane only through human agencies. With the cry goes the promise of sure reward for all who hear and obey.

Letters from the Teacher Vol I, p137

The Lodge of Masters is eagerly watching and waiting for the development of every avenue through which They can pour love and wisdom to enlighten the world in this its darkest hour, the hour that precedes the dawn of the coming day. The whole aim and end of this Movement is to help each individual Soul to find, not only The Christ within himself, but also the guiding hand of the Master. We cannot assure you that you will find Him, for many feel around in a darkness created by themselves and never touch the out-stretched hand. We can only say that the Teacher and Guide stands ready, close at hand, to guide and help you through this labyrinth of darkness into the light of the perfect day.

Letters from the Teacher Vol I, p8

Directions for physical exercises are never given by a Master of Wisdom except in a personal way, and in such a case they would be adapted to that pupil's ability and capacity, and to that pupil alone. . . . No Master would ever give to a pupil exercises of a physical nature that would be likely to overtax his capacity. The Masters of Wisdom know well the physical conditions as well as the spiritual development of each pupil, and the Law of Growth is always followed.

Letters from the Teacher Vol I, p16

It will be only through your own individual effort, your attitude of Soul, and the character of your life that will enable you to place yourself in personal, conscious touch with the Masters. It depends upon no personality but your own. Only when this interior communion is established can the pupil come face to face with his Guru. Of course this will take place upon the inner planes, but long ere this he will be carefully instructed as to the necessary steps, the necessary cautions to be observed; will be told how to recognize and treat false teachers and false teachings. The requisite preparation for such close, personal contact is a sincere and loving heart, a child-like confidence and trust, and a willingness to sit at the Master's feet and be taught. You are ready for personal help when you can recognize and accept the instruction when it comes. . . . This is the Law: Only he who asks can receive, because the asking opens the doors through which help can come.

Letters from the Teacher Vol I, pp20, 22, 26

CHAPTER 7

MISCELLANEOUS

Know well that no matter how lofty a philosophy may be, or how good a lesson, unless it brings to your individual Soul some practical application, something that you can work into your daily life, that philosophy is of no account to you.

Letters from the Teacher Vol I, p136

All teachings that bring to humanity knowledge of the higher truths, and that awaken an interest in spiritual development, are useful, but individual Souls need special lines of instruction. Some find help under one teacher, some under another, and if your Higher Self knows that the one from whom you are striving to learn is not the most helpful one for you, you will be impressed with a feeling of dissatisfaction. Yet this does not mean that the teachings you have been receiving are not excellent for a certain stage of growth, and just what you needed at one time. That which you need will appeal to you. One thing may appeal to you today and in a month or a year you may grow away from it. If you are sincere and earnest, this merely indicates that you have learned one lesson and must look elsewhere for the next. The great lesson to learn is to follow the leadings of your Higher Self and take for yourself what appeals to you and helps you. But be just as ready to concede to others the right to choose for themselves. . . . The oak does not continually reproach the violet because it does not try to be an oak.

Letters from the Teacher Vol I, pp114-115, 25

He who feels another's sorrow, who forgets self for others, has realized, in measure at least, the Divine.

The Voice of Isis, p73

Unless a teaching appeals to the heart and rings true to a Soul, it is not true to that Soul. . . . The fact that a teaching attracts and helps you is evidence that it contains the lessons needed by you for the step you are taking. The fact that a movement no longer appeals to you, no matter how helpful it may be to others, is evidence either that your Soul has learned the lessons that movement had for you, even though not mastered intellectually, or that the movement, no matter how beautifully conceived and launched, has become tainted with something that is not helpful, or is perhaps distinctly injurious to your physical, mental, moral or spiritual growth. To remain connected with an organization to which you no longer feel drawn, or which you have outgrown, is as detrimental to your Soul-growth as it would be for a flower to remain in a pot which had become too small for it, or whose soil had become exhausted or contaminated.

The Voice of Isis, pp424, 426

If you cannot find time to enter the Silence, still no power in heaven or earth can keep the Silence from entering into you if you will let it.

The Voice of Isis, p33

You will never find Truth in any teachings if Truth, to you, depends upon the perfection of the instrument through which that Truth is expressed. You must cultivate the power of spiritual discernment and not allow anything to turn you aside from Truth. Learn to seek Truth for Truth's sake. Look for it among the stubble and muck of life, and in the dark places where humanity crawls in filth; look for it hidden under the mountains of selfishness and self-sufficiency of teachers; seek for it as a Jewel of Great Price that has been lost; for you may find the Jewel where you least expect it. But first rise up and sweep your own house diligently.

Letters from the Teacher Vol I, pp141-142

Every fault is a virtue perverted and every hard circumstance of life is a stimulus to learn a needed lesson.

The Lord Jesus Christ, II, p3

As to failings, we all have them. The greatest example the world can have is to see a brave Soul struggling to do right. It is those who are honest with themselves; who know their own weaknesses, yet are striving to conquer; who recognize that they are not above their fellow men; who are capable of feeling a sympathetic thrill with every failing and can grasp a brother's hand and from the heart encourage him to struggle onward, because they themselves are still struggling, they are the ones who are the real examples.

Letters from the Teacher Vol I, p123

If you have a fault you wish to correct, create its opposite. Think no more about the fault, but put all your thought on its opposite. Put your failures behind you. Give them no more force by thinking of them or worrying about them. Live each day for itself, for if you can conquer one day at a time you conquer all.

Letters from the Teacher Vol I, pp101, 103

If the world's sorrow oppresses you, remember that the very best you can do toward lifting that heavy load is to make a centre of joy and gladness in your own heart. . . . The only way really to help humanity is to take hold of that morsel of humanity over which you have been given command (your various bodies and all pertaining to them, the portion of goods belonging to you, given to you by your Father ere you took your journey into this far country of earth-life) and begin by redeeming it. . . . This is the sure, in fact the only true way, to become an agent of the Masters. . . .

Letters from the Teacher Vol I, pp76, 121-122

If you study Hamlet, you will find that in his attempt to set the world aright he only brought sorrow and suffering to himself and those he loved, and sacrificed not only his own personality but also the personalities of others in his misguided attempt. No person has ever been born to set the world aright except so much of it as he finds expressed in his own personality. If you mind your own business and let the faults of others go, trusting to the Law to straighten them out, and confine yourself to straightening out your own faults, you will realize the joy that comes from such conquering. When you cease to worry over the faults of others, it will be like a physical burden rolling from your shoulders. If you have never done this, try it merely as a physical experiment for your own happiness and the results will prove its truth.

The Voice of Isis, pp95-96

If you were in a congregation which was singing out of tune, the best way to bring about harmony would be, not to stop the singing and talk about it, but to sing steadily and firmly in perfect tune yourself. Those next to you would catch and spread the harmony until all were singing in tune. It will be only the working out of this law of harmony that will ultimately redeem "the round world and all that dwell thereon."

The Voice of Isis, p97

Every Soul has implanted within it, as an integral principle, the power of intuition, just as every mineral, vegetable and animal has the power of selection or instinct, which leads it to follow the lines of evolution best fitted for its growth and perfection in accordance with its environment.

Letters from the Teacher Vol I, p27

Prayer is the Jacob's ladder, one end resting on earth, the other reaching into heaven. If you ask sincerely, in the Silence, for guidance, and if it is the real, sincere cry of the heart for help and light that goes out, verily your Father-in-heaven who heareth in secret shall reward you openly. Never has a sincere cry for help been sent out in the Silence, where God dwelleth, that was not answered. The thing to do is to recognize the answer when it comes. . . . True prayer or spiritual aspiration is simply a correlating of the brain and physical consciousness with the spiritual, thus creating a natural channel of communication through which the spiritual force can flow. In other words, it is closing the circuit. The Will, a desire for spiritual gifts, and a constant attitude of devotion are the proper channels, but words, meditation and a recognition of the end to be attained, are steps leading to the opening of them. To ask for guidance is but to take hold of the power of Divinity as a little child grasps its father's hand. The child does not say, "Father, give me bread and clothing and house-room"; for all that is its birthright; but it is quite right to come to its father with its difficulties, its lessons and its little tumbles and bruises and ask for sympathy and help.

Letters from the Teacher Vol I, pp29-30, 34-35

During the darkness, while we sleep, all the stored up energies of the invisible rays begin their cycle of activity and our bodies grow and put forth anew, according to the pattern we have set for our physical lives.

The Iron Age, pp3-4

Poise is the result of self-knowledge. . . . It is not stoical indifference to pain and pleasure, but rather rising above it. Poise is the ability to remain calm at the centre, and while recognizing and understanding both the greatest joy and the greatest sorrow, not be carried to either extreme. To enjoy intensely carries with it, as the opposite swing of the pendulum, the power to suffer to a corresponding degree. We never reach a point where the waves of force generated by the opposite poles, pain and pleasure, cannot reach us, but we can rise above them so they cannot sweep us from one extreme to another.

Letters from the Teacher Vol I, p123

Do not accept the teachings of any spiritual or occult movement until through prayerful consideration and meditation you receive the confirmation of your own Divine Guidance that it is the open door for your next step.

The Voice of Isis, p113

Coloured blocks are necessary in the kindergarten, primers for children, textbooks for the training of the mind in school and college; but when the mind has been trained it must then put that training to use in a practical way: in business, under the head of the firm or manager; in art, under a great teacher, in spiritual things, under a Master of Wisdom. But, remember that, because you are no longer interested in the coloured blocks or primers you once thought so beautiful; you are not to despise the children who still cling to them, or find fault with the teachers of the a-b-c's. All have their place, and the children will grow away from the blocks when they have learned their lessons, just as you have grown. The proof that you have outgrown earthly organizations will be the love and tolerance with which you treat all your brothers and sisters who still feel the need of such methods. To rail at organizations, especially one which has helped you to reach your present state, and those who work in them, is proof that you still need their discipline. Every uplifting movement or teaching has its place and has for followers those who need its lessons.

The Voice of Isis, pp426-427

A thing that costs you nothing is valued at nothing. Just in proportion to the real love and sacrifice will be the value to your own Soul. In other words, what we love we work for, sacrifice our time and money for. And out of those things, or their inner force, is our character built up.

Letters from the Teacher Vol I, p31

Under no circumstances can an evil or impure thing upon the earth-plane become anything but evil and impure on the higher planes, for all planes are one, and what is impure on one is impure on all. Under no circumstances can evil or impure acts on the physical-plane cause spiritual growth, for the acts themselves are creating exactly the opposite conditions. Those who are teaching such abominable doctrines under the name of Esoteric Theosophy or under the guise of obtaining some sort of spiritual development, will have a terrible Karma to answer for in the future. We cannot emphasize too strongly the fact that there can be no spiritual teachings, either esoteric or exoteric, that are not spotless in their purity on all planes, for The Christ can dwell only with the pure in heart.

Letters from the Teacher Vol I, p92

There is not a single man or woman who cannot be an active factor in bringing the Golden Age of Love, Peace, Harmony and Brotherhood into manifestation the sooner, through the controlling of thoughts, words, emotions, and by overcoming his or her resistance, and responding more and more understandingly and gladly, to the upward urge of the Divine.

The Philosophy of War, 1st Edition, p25

That which we fail to appreciate, the Great Law removes from us.

Letters from the Teacher Vol I, p72

There is no such thing as death, merely various *changes in form* in the manifestation of the One Life.

The Voice of Isis, p400

As long as there is motion, which is vibration or life, we cannot get away from God, for it is in this God that "we live and move and have our being." . . . . All that exists is substance, but in different rates of vibration.

The Message of Aquaria, p60

Nothing in the nature of man is inherently evil; it is only evil through its misuse and the evils that are attached to it. Determine to deliver it from evil and to find The Christ-force within every temptation and everything that assails you, knowing full well that these things are the portion of goods that have been given you by your Father at your request, your just belongings that you have deserved and out of which you must create your immortal habitation. Not one thing must be lost or wasted or destroyed, but each must be transmuted and its golden potency indrawn and built into the immortal Temple of the Living Christ. This is the meaning of the sentence in the Lord's Prayer, "Deliver us from evil."

Letters from the Teacher Vol I, p113

No matter what the apparent source of any teaching and no matter how beautiful the language used, do not accept it unless it meets the test of purity and commonsense, does not violate the moral code, and is confirmed by the intuition of your own Soul.

The Voice of Isis, p265

The greater the work laid out for a neophyte, the greater the necessity for thorough testing. This is a merciful law, for the suffering and the evil Karma would be much worse to bear if you were given a great opportunity and failed for lack of proper training; for, of necessity, you would draw others down with you. Until you have been tried and have proven your strength you cannot bring forth the harvest. . . . The greater the struggle, if persisted in to victory, the stronger and more self-reliant will be the new-born Soul.

Letters from the Teacher Vol I, pp117, 119

The true teacher must have evolved beyond the little personal self and to some extent merged his consciousness into the Divine, hence neither seeks nor permits adulation or worship for himself, but lets the Divine in him speak through his teachings.

The Voice of Isis, p133

The Christian Bible, like all great scriptures, is an inspired setting forth of the one Divine Wisdom in symbolic language. It deals with principles, not things. It describes qualities, forces and spiritual events, not historical men, places or physical events. It is "a repertory of invented personages in its older Jewish portions, and of dark sayings and parables in its later additions, and thus quite misleading to anyone ignorant of its esotericism." It is less understood than more ancient scriptures, because all so-called study of it has proceeded upon the hypothesis that it is intended to present historical facts. In reality, no great scripture is historically true, nor is it supposed to be by those who, having been initiated into its mysteries, understand something of their inner meaning. All scriptures and myths are collections of allegories and parables, grouped and arranged to illustrate symbolically some feature of the growth of the Soul. Hence, while not historically true, as modern research has abundantly shown, they are universally true, because they illustrate phases of experience through which every Soul passes during its evolution toward conscious union with the Divine. Whenever possible, familiar historical incidents, names and places are used to illustrate the points more clearly, and also to inculcate a moral lesson for "them that are without," i.e., not initiated, who are able to grasp only surface truths.

The Voice of Isis, pp75-76

Cultivate love and tolerance for all your brethren and avoid the thought that your way or your view is superior, or in any way better, than another's, except for yourself.

The Voice of Isis, p406

A hasty temper is like a fire; put it in a furnace and it will generate steam or force that will run machinery and accomplish a great work for the world. A sharp tongue, controlled, will be a weapon that can fearlessly cut the evil from the good; its ruler is love. Intellectual pride is a dangerous master, but a wonderfully efficient servant. Wed it to humility and let love bless the union.

Letters from the Teacher Vol I, p52

Every person belonging to a spiritual movement (as well as its leaders) is absolutely responsible for the force that enters the body of humanity through them, as well as for the force they bring into the movement.

The Voice of Isis, p113

There is no surcease for sorrow except when the heart rests in Divine Love, in the assurance that all is well; that there is no failure; that underneath the stormy waves of life there is a firm foundation; that the deep waters shall not overcome you, for your Loving Father has hold of your hand, and your understanding (feet) finds a sure resting-place on the rock of the Law beneath the waters.

The Fire of Law, p4

The animal nature, to be the servant of the Real Self, must be well taken care of, well fed, well-groomed and comfortable, but not over-fed or indulged. Thus taken care of the animal will do far better work and make far fewer demands than one that is starved or ill-treated. You need the animal for your servant; you need all its powers in their best possible condition. Therefore, treat it as you would any other finely bred animal of which you expected great intelligence and great service. The physical must be conquered and controlled, not killed out. Everything that you crush out and weaken must be taken up again and again until you perfect and do your full duty by it.

Letters from the Teacher Vol I, pp71-72

Nothing will so retard our own evolution as to steal from another that which has been given to him and not to us, be it a thing, a thought, an opportunity, or a life. . . . Evolution is retarded until humanity as a whole awakens to the importance of the fact that every Soul must have freedom of opportunity to find its own place, perfect itself in its work and follow out the inner guidance of its Father-in-heaven.

The Key to the Universe, pp303, 305

It is a mistake that is often made, and one that is fostered by the teachings of all the orthodox churches, as well as by many other organizations, that sorrow is the only road to purification; that to be miserable is meritorious and that only through scourging and suffering can we hope for salvation. The truth is that, when we realize how much sorrow there is in the world and know of a certainty that thoughts are things and that either joy or sadness has the power to spread over a large area, it becomes our duty to be joyful and happy.

Letters from the Teacher Vol I, p75

All is Law, and all Law is Love. Love in its highest expression is the one power which you possess in common with the gods. It is a divine force of attraction which seeks equilibrium in the union of the masculine and feminine expressions of the Divine.

The Voice of Isis, pp214, 216

Since scriptural stories and events do not agree with the proven facts of history (except incidentally, here and there), the Bible has either been accepted in a literal sense and slavishly followed, even against all common sense and justice, or it has been mutilated and only such parts as can, seemingly, be "proved" accepted, and the rest rejected or discredited. In studying the seemingly preposterous myths and legends of gods and goddesses found in more ancient scriptures, we have no difficulty in understanding that they are not supposed to have an accurate historical basis, even though referring to historical or astronomical events. We do not attempt to pin them down to actual facts, but seek for the hidden meaning pertaining to the spiritual development of mankind which we know they must contain. The Bible, instead of dealing with gods and goddesses, deals in exactly the same way with personages and places, some of which are taken from history, not because their use in this way pretends to be history, but because the historical facts readily lend themselves to the illustration of the lesson intended. Other names and places used are just as fictitious as those used in the ancient myths ; but they all have their inner, occult significance, the numerical value of the very words themselves have a definite meaning, and are purposely selected to indicate steps in the Path of At-one-ment up which each Soul must journey.

The Voice of Isis, pp76-77

Until you recognize Divinity speaking to you from every other atom of humanity; until you have ceased to seek out your brother's mistakes ; until you have ceased to look for his shortcomings and failings; ceased to measure his corn by your bushel of human frailty and have found how to use God's measure instead; until you have ceased to listen to the many voices of the world and begun to listen to the one Divine Voice manifesting through all humanity as through Nature, you will never hear the Silent Voice within.

The Soundless Sound, pp18-19

Even though we may be but the humblest of human creatures, still we have our lives to live, our place to fill, our record to make, and our grain of truth to leave behind.

The Message of Aquaria, pp261-262

www.ingramcontent.com/pod-product-compliance
Lightning Source LLC
LaVergne TN
LVHW010108110826
845155LV00028B/539

* 9 7 8 1 9 2 0 4 8 3 0 3 6 *